Relate

A Guide to Strong Relationships

[by A.R. Williams]

[Relate]

A Guide to Strong Relationships

[Relate]
A Guide to Strong Relationships

By: A.R. Williams

Isaiah5812 Publishing

ISBN 978-0-9835698-0-0

Copyright © 2006 Ahmad R Williams BDA Isaiah5812 Publishing

Left Blank Intentionally

DEDICATION

Is there one who understands me?

Is there one who can stand me?

The other half that completes me

The only one who can speck into my Soul

And pull out the greatness in my Spirit

The one who has my best in mind and heart,

The one who would spend eternity

Waiting for me, helping me

Us, in a deal that beats all deals, me and her in a love story called life.

When her life is tough I will be her superman, but even he can't read minds.

So we will have one Mind, one Soul, one Spirit, that rise and set like the sun.

We will have one heart that beats like drums on a beautiful African coast.

My queen here is your king

Where are you? Here is your king waiting on you to return. Our kingdom awaits us.

Our rule shall be great; our kingdom shall stand, forever in love, peace, and harmonious bliss.

This, our destinies entwine as our realities connect and worlds fuse into one.

To those that have Relationship challenges.

Acknowledgements

Jimmy C - the late night talks you are my plum line.

Eddy – Helping me to cultivate and sharpen my mind.

Many more along the path of my journey that brought me here.

Table of Contents

Dedication

Acknowledgements

Introduction

Self Worth

13 Mentality

14 Egocentric

15 Don't Change Me

16 Am I Blind

17 Security

18 Security in a Relationship

19 Caution on Rescues

23 Attraction of a Void

25 Infidelity

Relationship Worth

29 Communication

29 Keys to Communications

32 Compromise

39 Hindrances

40 Broken Heart

42 Baggage

46 Visions

Conclusion

48 All things must come two an end

49 Final Personal Philosophy

Introduction

This book is not to point out the lacks or inadequacies of one of the sexes oppose to the other. Men and Women are the same, they want the same, do the same to get it and run into the same walls. However, the person may be different and the upbringing might affect different people in different ways. We all know what we want yet when someone comes to us we turn them down because of the package, or the way it is understood from our perception. I feel that if a person dislikes a person then they should first, be honest with themselves about why they do not like that person, reasons such as clothing or financial status are materials that even if in place don't guarantee a strong relationship. There are much more to relating to a person than what they can do for us, or dates having to include a financial analysis. There are parts of a relationship that are the glue, which can make things flow like romance. Always flirt with your mate, be the one to always make your mate smile and they do the same for you, neither having to ask or having knowledge of the others intentions like, Surprise! Baby just got you the watch you <u>needed</u>. Communication is one of the most important parts of any relationship. Together you and your mate should be a driving force in unison accomplishing all goals that are

11

set, not just his, not just hers but all.

What you expect from your partner may not be what they expect from you. Sometimes the best way to say you love someone is by not saying anything at all. Just listen to their words and the manner of speech and you will hear their heart. With all the things in this world today how hard is it to have a steady, serious relationship. It seems impossible like a fairy tale or myth. Men cheat, lie, women cheat, lie and we get so catch up in who is to blame or who did what or didn't do what that we miss at times the lesson about us and our choices, and opportunities. Sometimes we look for the wrong qualities or traits. I had a relationship with this female for almost a year. She had a car, we got an apt together thinking it was going to work, and everything was great. The sex was great; we liked the same things, yet it did not work.
Our communication was weak, we fail to expressed what we really wanted and felt to each other and very important also, to ourselves. Together we were individuals. Individuals have their own fears, beliefs, wants, visions and views, etc. If we cannot open up with our mates, talk, and reason together how, can we live together? Reasoning is the rational, logical thinking and consideration of both views in interest, for a common goal. People always say communication

is the key but there are keys to communication as will be explained in more detail later. Now sit back play some soft music and immerse yourself in the keyhole of a strong relationship.

Self

Mentality/Character

This we can say is the reasoning or critical thinking of a person, or we can call it one's perspective. People think and process things according to their experiences and upbringing. Understanding falls under this, for if someone does not understand, then that person will be less willing to go along or consider the idea purposed. Let us look at this from this point of view, if my mate and I cannot reason or critically think to understand each other, than eventually we will not be mates. For strong minded or stubborn people this can be difficult, because it takes a person to put themselves in the shoes of another and see through their window to understand what they are seeing or feeling. Though at times we see our own views so clearly and are so passionate about them, we are close-minded to any other avenues that the other person's perspective may present.

An open mind uses caution and observation, weights all views, and chooses the best option for what they are aiming for. , this may or may not be the goal of the other person but with proper communication and reasoning one can determine what that person's goal is. When two people have an understanding of each other, being open to reason there is not much they will not have, do, or achieve. However, there are times when one mate may be unreasonable and can pursue unreasonable terms; at this one, it is suggestive to take five from either the conversation or maybe the relationship.

Egocentrism

      This means self-interest, self-centeredness, or self-concern what some may call conceited. Everyone has had egocentric thoughts or ideas. It is humanly natural to think about one's self before others; it is human nature, survival of the fittest. In a relationship, this can be very dangerous to the progress of the relationship. Although the quality of the relationship can help decide, anyone in an abusive relationship it is encourage being egocentric and selfish, getting help, and getting out.

The egocentric thinker puts himself or herself in the forefront of everything including the relationship or they will do what is best for them and not the relationship, thus their mate. It is as if the person's in the relationship with themselves and their mate's there for their needs only.

15

Don't change me

This is when one person decides consciously or subconsciously that they will change certain things about the other person. This is also a plan for failure in a relationship. Ok, understand that some things are understandable to change for instance if it has negative effects on their life or well-being. There was a person that had a passion to play music and to teacher others, his girlfriend at the time was not as passionate, so she constantly would try to pull him away and tell him he needed to leave music alone and get a regular job. So a few times he did, he got a job, good pay, good hours, benefits, but it never worked, it just was not for him. He was miserable, continuously fighting the call to music. So finally, he gave in to his music and they parted ways, she found what she felt and believed she wanted and later realized that it was not enough. The Musician continued to play and made a very decent living at it, started a school and married. Now with many different avenues of perception the perspective to point out is the fact that the musician tried to change and it did not work, because his mated wanted him to for whatever reason. Now if he did stay at the job and work, he may not have done the things he did and he would have been unhappy and dangerous to the progress of the relationship or the parties of the relationship (emotions always needs an outlet, no matter the emotion, which can be dangerous or deadly in some cases). If she was a bit more patience and supportive she would be enjoying his passion and may have found a love for it all her own. Now this does not mean that you have to let your drunk, drink, or your smoker smoke these things are health issues that need a supportive voice and counseling, not a demanding or controlling one.

Am I Blind?

There is scientific research that says that our brain processes one thing at a time. Therefore, if we are looking at two things we can only process one at a time. For one seeking a relationship if there are two or more persons of interest, remember your brain is processing them one at a time so getting all the information is detrimental, for there are subtle words, actions or unspoken responses that can alert you to the potential of failure or fire in that potential relationship. This can lead us to choose the wrong person at times, because we are processing the wrong information, shoes, type of car, appearance, clothes, money; we should look for attitudes, mentality, goals, etc and have clarity in our sights to accomplish our goals as well as help them accomplish theirs. It is suggestive to get to know all persons as friends and make the choice to excel when the time is right. Everything happens in its due season as long as we do what we need to prepare for the next season. That is to have the clarity of mind and emotions to look pass the distractions, fronts, materials and see the type of being inside.

Security

   The government list security as money, though it takes many forms.
Women and men use this as one of the traits when searching for a potential mate.
Security can be money, physical, emotional, or just implied. In addition, leaving a person feeling unsecured for too long, it can leave a void, which another may fill. This can sometimes cause more confusion and problems for the parties of the relationship. People need other people in their lives and sometimes those other people may be there for the wrong reasons. To secure your mate do what makes them happy as long as they make you happy.

Security in a Relationship

From observations most women, and lately men as well, this is in the top three things when looking for or getting to know a potential mate. Whether it is implied or uttered, the thought is "no money, no honey." It is also an aspect of manhood from a female's perspective thus a good provider. The male most capable of providing, is thought to be the one that brings in the most from the field. The way a person dress and carry them self's can be the difference between an inviting look and smile or smile and look away. Yet for some there is nothing wrong with that type of qualifying mates, although these persons often find themselves with the wrong person in the wrong relationship going the wrong way. Alternatively, the relationship can suffer when the financial security shifts to them.

Another perspective is those seekers that take a chance and start something with those who are less financially secure. It can go good when given the proper chance, work, and time to grow and learn. From what I've seen those who date or even sit and take time to deeply talk to the persons they would most lightly not go for, end up in healthy lasting relationships some friendly or romantic progressing into marriage (this also can include friends that long to be more). For instance, the guy who always goes for the model type or the female that always go for the thug type and wonder why it doesn't work. These are examples of the things that we may lack or have bad experiences with and now we sought to consciously or more often subconsciously secure with things from other people or the person themselves.

The moments that we start something with someone we do not want (usually it just happens) are when we find rare gems in the dirt that with the right attention will shine forever. Money helps and the lack of it can be a strain, but until we communicate, we may miss an opportunity to achieve what we have strived. They can be your King or Queen in a bad season or moving to their season or maybe need be rescue, which may in turn rescue you.

Caution on Rescues

1st get to know the person, and in stages as you see who they are, look at who you are and see if it is a fit on all levels. (Did not say as they show you who they are, because a person can show you, what you want to see doesn't mean it is the truth, but you will always see the truth. Do not mean you will act on that truth, as it may be too subtle. This is where clarity and an open mind helps, reasoning with reality (the person

and what you see) your mind pass (history) and future realities (what you want) Gradually get to know them and your comfort level will increase or decrease. Then you show each other more and more of who yourselves are, where you are and wish to go. Now you are building the foundation of all strong relationship types, a friendship. You know what you want and you can see what that person wants, so it is suggested to follow your instincts and be caution, not all that glitter is gold.
Some may say this does not apply to those entering into a sexual relationship, where sex is the only goal. There the focus should be on their sexual habits, health, and marital status not just their sexual performance. Although it still would suggest caution and do not strongly promote this type of relationship.

Have an open mind; an open mind is open to the potential positives, yet not over looking or undermining the obvious negatives often missed. In a relationship optimism can be a good thing, if it doesn't look good from the start be cautious but optimistic, hope for the best and prepare for the worst. Open minds are ready to absorb all the information around them. No matter how unimportant that information may seem an open mind while still monitoring changes and variations takes it into consideration that

21

information. It is important that an open mind be cautions and patience with very careful observation. When you meet someone, you can run the risk of being just a one night stand (unless that is what you want), or they can be a cheater, thief or something worst, remember intentions are not worn as a badge on the sleeve. Though open minded, careful not to move to fast but open to the possibility that this can be a good person and caution to the chance they may not.
A friend and I conducted a double blind social experiment with some strangers to research their behavior and responses (no one knew they were being researched for this project, I just found the results interesting and worthy of mention in this book).
One of the tests first was with a female that I had being interested in, at the time my appearance was ruff, I allowed my bread and mustache to grow, and clothes were causal, Dockers and a black-Tee.
I would come in to work on my laptop, sit in the back where I would be least bothered. A conversation between us started and we talked as if we had talked before and knew each other, then I ask a few questions. One question was how she viewed me from the time we did not speak at all to now. She said at first she thought that I was a bum, and then she thought that I was trying to sell my laptop. So I asked her what

22

point would she have considered a date with me and she responded by saying, "I would date you now that" and she stopped and walked away. Later she said that it was my appearance and perceived financial status, which was the foundation of her decisions, but when she had talked to me and realize there was more to clothes then the appearance, and me she realized she had made a mistake. At the time, there was another person that would come in from time to time. She showed him more, he showed her that he had money and dressed to her liking, which she later found out that he had a wife and kids and was cheating with her on the side.

Then a female I had date for a few years who felt it was time 4 someone else, stating I was not secure enough for her, did something that surprised me. She like many other females, kept a link to me in the event that my status would change and when a hint or sign that it did, she would make contact inquiring of my financial status and at times marital status.

I continued and found that when I went to a few places, just to get a different crowd of people around me. Some of the females did not even want to look at me and those that knew me acted as though I was not there, clearly on my appearance. So the moment I got a haircut (I mean a $12 barbershop cut not a free do-it-yourself, all must go bathroom cut) changed clothes and the response was the total opposite. I was called over to sit with people, I was included in conversations and even regarded as one of the posse but later on as the hair grew back and the money and clothes was gone so was the welcome. In the pursuit to learn more me and my cousin found riding together one night that a car of females paid more attention to him driving as if I wasn't there, than to both of us. He also explained his observations of similar results. I do not say this to say that it is wrong to worry about money or appearance in your mate, but that should not be the initial thing or the one thing alone that disqualifies them or stops you from talking to a person.

Attraction of a Void
     One day my Uncle said to me in the course of writing this book that, he believed that there is something in all of us that attract the wrong people no matter how much we may want that dream person; we get the opposite or the worst of the choices. I agree and feel that there is more to this than just what the line states. Many believe that as human beings we are beacons that transmit certain energies. So, how is it that we would not transmit what we do not want, or is it that we focus on what happen last time so much that our subconscious feels that it

24

is what we are aiming for? On the other hand, maybe it is that it comes to us in so many different forms; we do not recognize or identify the traits and habits of a potential mate that we do not want. Possibility it could be that we focus on what we do want so much that we blind ourselves from what we have found, not considering the negatives or subconscious beliefs that hinder us from taking a chance but overlooking them. At times, our friends can play an important part in this where they can be and often are the objective voice when we venture into something new. Yet, that opens questions on the strength and position of that friendship, where jealousy can rise or be present. I have seen in situations where friends of mine have asked me for advice about the new person in their life at that time. I gave them the insight from what information I gather, what they have told me about the person and the way they interact with each other or from what I witnessed. I have given the advice to step back, leave it alone, or to go for it and what brought me to my conclusions, yet my advice was not considered or put into motion which lead to, in some cases, very hurtful results. I am not stating this to show my great insight into this and wine that no one listens to me but to shed light on what is happening. I also found myself in the position of the hard headed or inattentive friend and my results were very similar, which cost me time to deal with it and to recover from it. I also am not saying to take everything your friends say as gospel and run with it but to again have the open mind and truly consider it as an observation and objective possibilities that can save you a lot of time and hurt. It is your decision what you do with that information but it is also better to consider it first, than act, oppose to act than consider or wish you had.

Infidelity
This is a void, weakness, or insecurity. It can be a void of understanding of how one mate displays feelings or is feeling. It can also be a void of physical or emotion fulfilling that one mate may want but do not receive and do not know how to ask or explain it. It can also be that one mate refuses to perform certain task to or for their mate. At times even the lack, increase or the performing to their mates liking in areas all can result in that mate going elsewhere for the filling of that void.
Some use it as a means to escape the present unwanted situation that they are in and others may find that it is a longing within a void that needs to be filled. All and all infidelity is and always will be a relationship breaker some get

more chances than others will will will and some get one. From observation, communication leading up to this time can be dull, lacking, or non-existent. The goal here is to learn your mate and what they need and want, and give it to them, leaving no reasons for them to want to leave or cheat, although some still do and that is the out pouring of resolved personal issues in them.

I often look at other couples and wonder to myself, they look so peaceful and in love but what transpires when hard times hit or they are behind clothed doors (that is a measuring stick of the growth of a relationship, when no one is around or looking and a problem is amiss? Do they sit down and talk or do they yell? Does he get mad and storm out the house or does she? What if there are kids involved, what are they seeing? Their parents lack of communication skills or good communication. I do not mean to focus so much on this but communication is one of if not the most important pillars of a relationship. The way you communicate with your mate should be unique and happen with no other person. The two of you should be of one mind, and of course, this comes over time with proper communication, understanding and reasoning, any problem can be solved. No one knows what the other person is thinking until that person speaks or acts so therefore be careful that act can damage the relationship. In that talk there may be things that may not come out, because as humans we often feel embarrassed, ashamed or that they are stupid and don't matter but remember what is important or unimportant maybe the opposite to your mate. Sometimes we may think that the other person will react in a negative way making us feel worst. A suggestion here would be to write them a letter and leave it where they can find it. Men include a rose or her favorite flowers, women you can put it under his favorite dish from his favorite restaurant, be creative, and make sure it is something that matters to them or something they wanted, they will appreciate it. In this letter, you can be as liberal and free as you want and you have had time to calm down, really take a good look at both views, considering how stubborn some can be. Relax you don't have all the answers and any relationship that is worth anything takes time and effort so consider what is being said, remember, you love this person and of course they love you. This is why you bought this book to seek answers; really, you have them all if you pay attention, see them and answer the questions about your present relationships bumps.

**Relationship
Worth**

29

Communication

Keys to communication

This is one of the main pillars in the fabric of all relationships, communication. In the Roget's II Thesaurus, the definition is "The exchange of ideas by writing, speech, or signals." Its synonyms are listed as communion, converse, intercommunication, and intercourse. How you communicate with any person can predict the level or quality of your relationship with that person. The communication between a husband and wife is different between friends, boyfriend, and girl friends and family. It can be as deep as looks or touches or as simple as a word or movement. Communication is one of the unique things about all species. I can still communicate thoughts, intentions, likes, dislikes etc even if I do not speak the language.

The communication between two beings in love should be so deep that words may not always be needed. It can be said that the two communes with each other and their spirits connect.

There are ways to improve communication, one you can just learn the language and that will take you so far. We must understand that there are stages of communication that I call keys, because with a key you can open doors. With these keys, you can open the doors to a great relationship. These keys are as follow:

30

Listening

This is the first step to communication. You have to hear what is communicated to you and with undivided attention absorb what is being transmitted to you. Pay attention to the words used, the phrasing, the Infosys, and the body language, the setting or environment all has its part in communication, because they reinforce the message being transmitted.

Understanding

Sometimes we may not grasp the fullness of the message being transmitted. This can lead to miss communication and thus ruin a relationship or create unnecessary hard times. Here as they say in school if you do not understand stop me and ask a question. You should never be afraid to ask a question. We all interpret and express things differently, questions creates bridges so that everyone is on the same page.

Reasoning

Many times, we do not reason with each other we argue, our point, to the point that one person walks away or things get physical. Reasoning is thinking, analysis, logic, calculation, reckoning, or interpretation. All these words take time in the performance of action. An example of a couple that reasons is one that sits and talks things through. If an agreement is not came to then an agreement to disagree has been made and maybe a compromise, now the reasoning process for some couples may take hours, days or even weeks for some it takes lifetimes and they realize oh that was what my mate was saying. So in essence, this stage of communication is first personal, we reason with in our minds the thoughts about people's actions or words and things that just don't add up or sit right with us based on our beliefs and experiences. A part of reasoning and being able to maybe compromise is to know the wants of the other person and understand them.

Response
 This stage is a floating stage, which means it can fall anywhere but the proper place for it is after reasoning, because any other place usually results in a surgically removing a foot from their mouth. A response may also come a while later as a person may need more time to reason through before they can understand what they heard. This does not include questions they would be a part of understanding as one may question to understand what they heard.

Compromise

A compromise is the molding of conflicting interests to satisfy the interests of the involved parties, for the best satisfying result. This is a result of good communication. There are Compromises and excuses and for too long we excuse ourselves and compromise the wrong things as we learned to. We compromise our hearts for pleasure, our happiness for fame and our joy for shallow phantoms. We compromise for the wrong things money, love of the wrong things yet for a relationship in our hearts is true. We don't want to but one day we may look back in our minds and say what happen I am nowhere near where I wanted to be or even I am actually where I always wanted to be but for some reason not happy or fulfilled. Why is that?
Compromise is a part of life that we often neglect and rarely properly utilize. Who can see the future but wise men say it is in our hands if we only grasp it, without compromising ourselves and losing the essence of which we are what we hate or dislike which we sometimes are to become.

Women; the level of morality is growing lower and lower and a lack, thereof has become the norm for women in this day. How is it expected for a man to accept a woman, if he can ask his friends or anyone around any and everything he wants to know about her sexually, it entails no morals? It really is not cute and is not that important to get laid. Try the person you think is lame, isn't dressed right, talk different, walk different, you make find that what you thought about that person is quite the opposite and find what you are really longing subconsciously.

Listen to your man when you have one and support him, keep him grounded, don't try to understand it all at once in your way but try to understand him and his way, with love, and reasoning all else will fall in place. For those women that pursue security above all, careful, money will not buy you love, but the man that truly will love you will secure you. Treat your man like your king and you will be treated like his queen forever (only work if you find a king not a joker). Do not blame him for things that go wrong, look, and see how the two of you can fix it even if it is his fault, he knows and if he is a real man, he will say it in his own way. Blaming don't bring solutions or strengthen the relationship, it stresses and strains until your home girl is comforting your man, straight to her bed room and your mad at him. Look in yourself first and how you handled things before he leaves. A good man wants a good woman as must as she wants a good man. After you have looked at yourself, cooled off, so you do not lost your composure or clear perspective of the situation then present it to him.

Now as far as the bi-curious, bi, and lesbian females, It can said that some of you love the femininity of a female and others well for all the wrong things men have done, you are just cold and angry cause some guys were idiots and did you wrong. Not all guys are bad; there are still some good ones out there. So what is the difference between a female and male? A split and pole, the feeling, sensuality, taste, smell, I can go on but in the end you still can get hurt or used either way and we were not created to do those things. If homosexuality is from birth, well I know a lot of exceptions, people who have tried it, done it and moved on to the opposite sex and are happy together and never looked back. It is all, desire introduced by pleasure or loneness, not fitting in and a reaction or personal dealing of things that traumatically shaped emotions, feelings and changed preferences.

Multiple partners are multiple opportunities for disaster. With STD's running amuck, I would rather use my hand or a toy. That goes for one-night standers as well. Phone sex it is a desire, if you let it control you then you are a slave to it and who ever can make your feel the best. It all ties your soul to the desire or to the love of that desire, supported by pleasure. Desire is like a tree, the more you feed that desire oppose to another the more it grow and gains strength to the point that it becomes a habit and sometimes more often than not you love the pleasure, than its off to find yourself stuck in that one place feeling empty and dry.

    I was told a defensive tool used by women is the "I got a man" line maybe true for some but either way it is often a reflective turn down or a deterrent from being asked for their number. Well this is normally the case if the guy is not in the image they want with money, clean-shaven, new clean shoes, nice clothes. Now from this most if not all women would say, "Well I don't want no broke man that I have to take care of" or the "not my type" line mean he is not where I would want him to be. Now this is on the 1st meeting usually and a decision is made but what if that guy moves up a level he changes to a new type all of a sudden he becomes a women's dream man or now he is worthy of some extra attention.

Well the truth can be seasons, if you catch a man in his bad season and say oh wait he's not there yet clothes are off, shoes dirty, pockets low or empty and you brush him off thinking next where are the ballas. The ones with the nice car, the house, a job or real job as some put it and money in the bank or their pockets which that might be his season but just as seasons change people's seasons change and tonight a 0 might be

36

a 10 tomorrow or a month, week or with your input, presence, words, assistance or even attention he can become an 1000 but the thing is the 1000 can turn out to be an 100 when you wake up the next morning or a wk, month or year later. What a man wear drive or have in his pockets, do not make the man. Where he is, at that moment maybe only a step along the journey of where he is going. Therefore, ladies, be very careful that you do not miss your king on an egocentric technicality or patty materials. Yes it would be easier to have a man with something but if the man isn't enough for you without the things it limits you as a woman also if he loses it all it means you have to find something else about him you like.

Men; your women should be the queen or your heart and not the prize of your pursuit for pleasure and vain praise from the boys. Women are your legs when you cannot walk, your heart when it skips a beat, the rib that you are missing, to fulfill you and support you in the building of a family. Men, you are the foundation and the woman is the walls, how is the house to stand if the foundation is broken, weakened, lost, chasing cheap thrills that land you in places unthought-of in your worst dreams. It is not wrong to love and to show it to carry a moral stick that you measure yourself and strive for your goals. Men compete with each other for unnecessary reasons and things, compromising their strength, pride, and dominion. It is time for the men to stand up; we have women being men to boys and boys thinking they are men or women. We are losing the foundation of manhood and compromises for a watered down arrogance with no wisdom or purpose. Whenever men fell to be men or when the foundation of a house fell to be a foundation, the house falls so what purpose then, does the foundation have? Is it to be beat by the rains of life and shattered by the weather? Your woman will shelter you with her love and nurturing spirit, keeping you grounded and focused to achieve your destiny, but only if she is treated as the queen she is and not the trash that some boys have taught her to think she is.

It has been said that men are scare of commitment, maybe they are scare of what they are committing to and the pain and lost that it can bring if broken or not what they thought it would be. Some men find it very difficult to be in deal with emotional situations. They take it hard being the less emotionally displaying of the two sexes. When a guy is hurt it is harder for them to contain, control and recover, than a

38

female. Females can hurt and not show it but only the closes of friends can recognize it, guys become wrecks, they shut down, it is a short circuit in the programming that made that man. The programming that says men do not cry or show their emotions. It has become the hard wiring of manhood. Some men learn to control, channel their emotions, and let them out in their own way or they come out and if bottled up for a long time can be explosive. One way to comfort the emotions of a man, first, carefully identify them, like a bike tire when it has a hole you patch it and sometimes you need help to patch it and sometimes too many holes might be a clue o get a new one (tire or man). Do not judge him or make him feel that you are, caress the ego and express what you love and see in him. Build him up.

One way to identify a man's emotions truly depends on the man. Some can hide them very well but a woman that learns her man can see them. Sometimes a woman can see them and not know how to fix them or is unwilling to give up something or do something to fix them. It may be insecurities from a pass or it can be a wound that has not being dealt with and allowed to heal. The first thing is to learn your man again; I say learn your man and men learn your women. What they like, dislike, what makes them happy, sad, sick, or angry. It is best you console and talk with them, strengthening the bond between you. You can also be firm for the hardheads if necessary, but as you learn them you will know when to. (No hitting from either of you) when working through this it's the two of you and no one else unless you can't resolve it then professional help may be needed or time a part, it does make the heart grow fonder.

Hindrances

Stubbornness can be very detrimental to a relationship where one might have a good point and the other is being too stubborn to consider or accept it. As one whom wants to leave the relationship for unreasonable purposes and the other who does not want them to go. Or one who wants to buy something and other wants to save the money. Many of the things in Mentality can also be a hindrance not only to find a good mate but also to excel in life itself.

40

Broken Heart

The heart is needed to live; it is a very strong and important organ that does not compare to any other organ because it has a main needed function, to pump blood throughout the body. When we talk about the heart in the context of a relationship, the roles are very similar. Think of a relationship as the body. Communication is the blood of a relationship and sex the part of the adhesive that helps the bond of the relationship. If there is, no blood the body dies, if there is no communication the relationship dies. If there is no sex, there is no release or good sex no good release and maybe a thin layer of adhesive stick. The heart is the pump in this process it articulates what comes in through the blood. Therefore, when something is said or done it travels through the blood. The heart than articulate what is said which can be dangerous because the hearts function is just that it has no way of knowing what is good or bad for the body but it just pumps whatever comes through it. Therefore, it can be difficult for some to deal with the heart and affairs of the heart, for when you love, like or crust on someone it is just that. The heart shows us the strength of love and what we love and can blind us from potentially dangerous

things coming from that love. In essence, we may love a person or care for a person that is no good for us and we do not see it until it is too late, despite the various warnings that may come. For instance the girl that likes the guy who just wants to sleep with her and that is it, she may not see that that is all he wants until after it has happen a few times and he is tire of her and is ready to move on. Or the female that likes the bad boy that is always in trouble, which ends up getting her pregnant, and leaves her, goes to jail, or dies. We must always guard our hearts because we are the only ones who truly know what it feels and what comes through it affects us. Just as we go to the doctor for a checkup, we must constantly check our hearts. The time will come when there is someone who we can trust with our hearts and we know they will treat it as their own.
I make efforts to reframe from using the term or phrase "fall in love" or falling in Love" because if you fall you have little or no control of yourself and where you land, and it is usually inevitable to get hurt. Love is a journey and you do not fall into a journey you undergo a journey so "grow in love" for as you walk on a journey you grow to the terrain and weather with the person you undergo the journey. It is true in movies certain hardships and struggles bring people together sometimes for the good or bad but you have

more control. It is like trying to run through a wall instead of climbing over it.

Baggage

Some people do not recognize that they have baggage and some do not see that their mate does. There are different levels of baggage for some, love hard and fall hard and some have no heart figuratively speaking. Everyone has baggage some pile it in a closet of their heart or mind and others carry it like a badge on their chest, it is one of the things that shape our dating habits or our acceptance of what we will and will not deal with in the relationship, and how we interrupt the actions of our mate.

Thinking about the relationships, I have had and how they affect me, brought me to this conclusion. I was thinking about a friend of mind and the events and duration of our friendship. We would constantly text each other and at times call for brief converses. When in person we slept together and talked about having a stronger relationship or going to the next level. I was still hung up on many of the things that happen between me and my ex, which hindered the relationship from prospering into what it could be. So it fell, they went their way and I mine, now we barely text or talk and when we do it is a loud silence that deafens us and drives us away.

There was a time we were having a good conversation, until I ask about her sexual escapades after the last time we had done anything, the conversation died and she never responded. The next day I thought about it and strive for an answer then I realize my baggage had driven her to another. One piece of baggage I see often is when it pains a person to realize that they can't choose the outcome no matter how much they may wish that their ex is sleeping with another person or giving them something that was once exclusively theirs, still holding on to the pass can be heavy baggage that even the strongest of relationships cannot bear. Which lead me to the conclusion that they are not the end, not the end of love, or the last relationship or friend, I shall love again as shall you, now say it again "I Shall Love Again." The person that we had done things with or wished that we had is not a speck on the person that we shall end up. Obviously, an ex is an ex for a reason and if there is no grounds for reconcile then it is best to look to the future, for that is where the healing can start and that person will arrive, once you have dealt with the baggage that you are or maybe carrying from one relationship to another. It may be easier for some than it is for

44

others but the truth is that it must be done.

    When a relationship is broken or damaged, the toll can be taken on both parties for a lifetime unless properly and timely dealt with. Another friend of mine I have had the chance to be a leaning tower to throughout the rise and fall of many of their relationships sexual and romantic. I strive to understand the reasoning in the romantic choices she made. I found a pattern that, from a young age she would carry baggage and store it until the situations raised and again and again she would get hurt and don't know why. Yes, there has grown a great deal of feelings for this friend romantic and friendly, yet it only brought me pain as I strived to be a friend and one day maybe more in the struggle to deal with their baggage and also my own.

One day it seemed that I understood a portion of their thinking, yet still confused. I realized that all the baggage had changed their mindset. They explained that I was not their type yet it seemed that the type they picked ended up using and abusing them leaving them with even more baggage and pain. This time the damage was taken out on me but they never considered my advice because it was perceived to be useless and basis because of my feelings, it also carried less weight in meaning than others because of my appearance and financial showings which came from pass baggage that was never resolved. I feel and understand that the things we hold as disqualifying factors against other people can be the things that hinder us from taking advantage of or utilizing the wisdom and knowledge or insight of those very people. Baggage can rob us of an opportunity or the person that will make us the happiest, it blinds us, I gathered this from the list of traits that they wanted in a mate and the traits later that they explained they saw in me or other people they disqualified for various egocentric reasons, they were the same but looking thorough the focus of their baggage did not see that.

I found that after the end of anything that involves emotions, the heart or the soul from a sexual tie point of view will require a time of restoration and discovery. Restoring yourself to the person you want to see and discovering the things that you have learned and experienced. Accepting the results if it is not in your power to change and reestablishing the personal goals that give you strength and makes you smile. I call it "dating your-self." In many instances that I have counseled I found that it can help to regain whatever was lost and to let go of the unchangeable. Dating yourself is basically what it is go out to eat, buy yourself a gift, take yourself to the movies or the beach and just enjoy you, appreciate yourself and you will realize though it may hurt, the pain will pass and the thoughts will fade and a new day shall dawn. They are not your end.

<u>Visions</u>
      We have been taught to be individuals and so when any type of relationship that we are faced with we face it as individuals with individual visions and we continue to pursue our individual visions as does the other members of that relationship. As the two people become one, the individual visions should also become one and merge into one vision that strengthen the relationship and supports both individual visions.
If not this can create conflict, because one may feel the other is being selfish or do not care about what they feel or want and can cause the two to drift apart. It is a structure failure of communication and compromise. Now one may not know the others vision or how to merge it or compromise it for the accomplishment of both and that can be worked out as the relationship is built. This is something that is conveyed with in the first stages of getting to know the character and mentality of each other once a relationship is formed then it becomes a process that can and should develop as the relationship does.

Conclusion

48

Putting it all together

The Roget's II Thesaurus describes a relationship as referred back to relation, being a logical or natural association between two or more things (i.e. mother, father, son, and daughter). The Synonym that I chose for the best fit for this book is interdependence. A relationship is logical and natural. Logical, meaning thought of reasoning, to be interdependent you have to be able to reason, a trait we often neglect when choosing our mates. Association is the state of being associated. A state or stage which entails' growth and a process with various different levels and on each level something to learn and deal with. Synonym is alliance. These are some tools or traits to strive for in your relationships. So in essence, you and your mate form an alliance where you logically reason to navigate through the obstacles on the intricate journey of interdependence called love.

A good relationship starts with a friendship a friendship starts and grows with loyalty, honesty, dedication and trust. Of course there are those things that are unforgivable for some yet there is also the understanding of how people interact with each other especially those in the relationship. First there must be communication

between the two and that communication should be without the limitation of anger. Anger clouds judgment and makes the next steps difficult, impossible or in the wrong direction, so it is best to communicate when both parties have calm down and can sit and talk not yell.
The next step is reasoning which is when two or more people can listen and consider the next person's perspective and not only their own, so a decision can be agreed upon or a compromise can be reached for the forward movement of the alliance.

Final Personal Philosophy

I feel that there really isn't "the one" or the perfect one for in this world what is perfect? But I feel there are matches that are good and bad and there are those that work and you work on it. Love is a journey. There will always be something, the good things usually turn out to be nightmares and the nightmares turn out to be fantasies at times. So work on you, what is good and bad with you from your perspective also considering what others have said about you, look from all angles it's you good or bad it's u. Change what you need to and fix what you should but do not change who you are for no one

50

but you.

Some have been sadly mistaken with the results of this mentality but do not recognize its pressure. In a relationship sparks can fly and all can be put into put place with the right person but who is to say that person would be on the levels that you want them on when you meet them, maybe you are the catalysis to motive them to the greatness they are going or visa-versa.

People usually have persons in their life that like them romantically and they don't like them that way. I also have experienced this and came to the conclusion that if I would have given that person a chance things that were not attractive to me make have changed or I may have seen attractive traits that I first missed or neglected to look for because of what I thought I was looking for, like a piece of coal apply the right elements of heat and you have one of the most valuable jewel in the world. At times it's the same with people, when we first meet them they maybe out of season or just entering, filled with wisdom that we need.

After Word

This book was written to give a foundation or help to those that may have troubles or those that feel lonely or feel that there is no one for them. This is to help understand some of the things that come against a relationship. All relationships should be based on the relationship that God wishes to share with us, whereas there is communication from the heart and a connection that is unique and determination to work through all things. The author does not make any notion or suggestions that they are any expert or authority but only share observations and understandings from various areas of personal observations. Moreover, as they say in show biz results may vary. LOL!

www.ingramcontent.com/pod-product-compliance
Lightning Source LLC
Chambersburg PA
CBHW051718040426
42446CB00008B/949